Let's Move It!

What Makes Things Move

(For Kiddie Learners)

Speedy Publishing LLC
40 E. Main St. #1156
Newark, DE 19711
www.speedypublishing.com

Things are in motion
all around you

When something is in
motion, it is moving.

Things may move in different directions.

An object may move in a straight path.

It may move in a curved path.

It may go in a circle.

It may even move
in a zigzag.

Motion makes the world go ‘round. Motion makes the moon go ‘round too.

Motion is important to our lives and impacts so many things that we do.

Motion is the changing of position or location.

But motion requires a force to cause that change.

Force is just a fancy word for pushing or pulling.

Force makes things move or, more accurately, makes things change their motion.

Two natural forces that we have experienced are the force of gravity and magnetic forces.

Objects move at different speeds; some move faster and some move slowly.

Speed is how fast something moves.

40

When we think of motion we often think of cars, bicycles, kids running, basketballs bouncing and airplanes flying.

But motion is so much more!

www.ingramcontent.com/pod-product-compliance
Lightning Source LLC
LaVergne TN
LVHW060833170826
845678LV00010B/1972

* 9 7 9 8 8 6 9 4 5 2 4 1 2 *